Every effort has been made to ensure the accuracy of the information in the first edition of this book, published in 2023.

Here are some of the sources used for this book:

6–7 How long have people been around for?
https://ourworldindata.org/human-height
https://www.who.int/data/gho/data/themes/mortality-and-global-health-estimates/ghe-life-expectancy-and-healthy-life-expectancy

8–9 Do you think the world is a crowded place?
https://www.worldometers.info/world-population/#pastfuture
https://ourworldindata.org/world-population-growth
World Population Growth, 2013, Max Roser, Hannah Ritchie, Esteban Ortiz-Ospina and Lucas Rodés-Guirao
https://worldpopulationreview.com/world-cities/tokyo-population

24–25 Has Earth's temperature changed?
https://climatekids.nasa.gov/kids-guide-to-climate-change/
https://climate.nasa.gov/evidence/
https://earthobservatory.nasa.gov/world-of-change/global-temperatures
https://www.imperial.ac.uk/media/imperial-college/grantham-institute/public/publications/briefing-papers/Sea-level-change-Briefing-Note-1v2.pdf
https://royalsociety.org/topics-policy/projects/climate-change-evidence-causes/basics-of-climate-change/

26–27 Has this progress been good?
https://bigthink.com/the-future/how-will-humans-change-next-10000-years/
https://www.nasa.gov/feature/artemis-iii
https://www.nasa.gov/content/nasas-journey-to-mars

28–29 A timeline of human history
https://www.southampton.ac.uk/~cpd/history.html
https://www.explainthatstuff.com/timeline.html
https://humanorigins.si.edu/human-characteristics/humans-change-world

Homo sapiens (human beings like you and me) have been around for about 300,000 years. This time span of human history is vast, so to make it easier to understand, we have condensed 10,000 years of human achievement into 100 days. The early dates are approximate as they are the subject of on-going research. In the conversion to 'days', some of the dates are rounded to the nearest hour or day for simplicity.

First published in Great Britain in 2023 by Red Shed, part of Farshore
An imprint of HarperCollins*Publishers*
1 London Bridge Street
London SE1 9GF
www.farshorebooks.co.uk

HarperCollins*Publishers*
Macken House, 39/40 Mayor Street Upper
Dublin 1
D01 C9W8

Text copyright © HarperCollins*Publishers* Limited 2023
Written by Jackie McCann.
Illustrations copyright © Aaron Cushley 2023
Aaron Cushley has asserted his moral rights.

Consultancy by Carole Stott and Dr Mike Goldsmith.
With thanks to William Jones.

ISBN 978 1 4052 9982 4
Printed in the UK by Bell and Bain Ltd, Glasgow.
001

A CIP catalogue record for this book is available from the British Library.

All rights reserved. No part of this publication may be reproduced, stored in a retrieval system, or transmitted, in any form or by any means, electronic, mechanical, photocopying, recording or otherwise, without the prior permission of the publisher and copyright owner.

Stay safe online. Any website addresses listed in this book are correct at the time of going to print. However, Farshore is not responsible for content hosted by third parties. Please be aware that online content can be subject to change and websites can contain content that is unsuitable for children. We advise that all children are supervised when using the internet.

Farshore takes its responsibility to the planet and its inhabitants very seriously. We aim to use papers from well-managed forests run by responsible suppliers.

Written by Jackie McCann

Illustrated by Aaron Cushley

IF OUR WORLD WERE 100 DAYS

RED SHED

How long have people been around for? Modern human beings like you and me (called *Homo sapiens*) have been around for roughly 300,000 years. For most of that time, life was completely different to the way it is today. People spent most of their lives looking for food, seeking shelter and protecting themselves and their families from wild animals. That all changed *c.10,000 years ago.

In the last 10,000 years, humankind has made incredible achievements that have changed the course of our history. But 10,000 years is a long time to imagine. To make it easier, welcome to our world of 100 days, where each day represents 100 years, and one hour equals roughly four years in the real world.

Let's begin with human beings – have we changed much in that time? Our ancestors were shorter than us! Eating better food and having more of it means that the average person is now taller. This is true for every country in the world.

100 days ago
men and women were shorter

The average man was about 166 centimetres tall and the average woman was 150 centimetres.

c. is short for 'circa', which comes from Latin and means 'approximately'.

People live longer than ever before. Thanks to better hygiene, modern medicine and vaccinations that fight disease and infection, fewer children die today, and the average adult lives for more than 73 years.

TODAY
men and women are taller

Today, the average man is around 171 centimetres tall and the average woman is 159 centimetres.

If we focus on a timeframe of 100 days, it's easier to picture how slowly, or quickly, human achievements have happened. Let's find out more about how life on Earth has changed and shaped us.

Do you think the world is a crowded place?
Today, there are more than 8 billion people on the planet. One hundred days ago, the world must have seemed quite empty as there were only about 7 million of us. The population explosion has been spectacular, but when did it happen, and how?

Our early ancestors are called hunter-gatherers because they moved from place to place, fishing, hunting wild animals, and gathering nuts and berries. They lived in small family groups, sheltering in caves or tepees made from animal skins.

100 days ago
7.24 million people on Earth

Eventually, people settled down and built permanent homes. They grew crops and kept cattle, which gave them a supply of food that was reliable. This was the beginning of what we call the 'agricultural age'.

Villages grew into towns and a few cities sprung up, but the world's population grew slowly. Many children died of disease or infection, and most adults didn't live longer than 40 years. Two days ago, the number of people on Earth hit 1 billion for the first time. After that, thanks to advances in medicine and better food, the population exploded!

2 days ago
1 billion people on Earth

1 minute ago
8 billion people on Earth

In the last two days, the world population has expanded rapidly due to better health and hygiene, and greater food supplies.

Today, more than 60 per cent of the world's population lives in Asia. Tokyo, the capital of Japan, is home to more than 37 million people and is the most populated city in Asia.

Does your home feel modern to you?

There may be lots of rooms, filled with things that make your life easier and more comfortable. But have you ever looked at the cooker, the fireplace, your bed or the bath and wondered if children long ago had these things too?

Our homes may be old and made of traditional materials, or built using the latest technology, but they have a lot in common with homes from thousands of years ago: they are places where we eat, sleep, wash and live with our families.

The first beds were built c.100 days ago in ancient Turkey. They were simple stone platforms, designed to keep the sleeper safe from scuttling insects and mice.

Plato, a philosopher in ancient Greece, invented an alarm clock that used water and dropping pebbles to wake the sleeper (c.24 days ago).

The first flushing toilet was probably used c.37 days ago in the Palace of Knossos in ancient Greece. Most people throughout history pooed outside!

The first permanent homes were simple, mud-brick houses, with a room in the centre and a clay oven for cooking and warmth. This area become the kitchen – the heart of the home.

Drinking chocolate is as delicious today as it was c.53 days ago, when people of the Mayo-Chinchipe culture in Ecuador drank it.

100 days ago homes heated by clay ovens

Some houses have a study: a room where people read and work. There may be a table and chair, with pens and paper. These things were all used in ancient Egypt c.25 days ago.

László Bíró, a Hungarian inventor, was behind the success of the first ballpoint pen, c.22 hours ago.

Around 11 hours ago, personal computers went on sale. Now, most people write on a keyboard, connected to a computer and the internet.

Toilet paper was first used c.14 days ago, in ancient China.

The people of the Harappan Civilisation in the Indus Valley in Pakistan invented plumbing. They built an enormous bath c.50 days ago that was probably used for bathing before or after religious events.

Ancient Egyptians cleaned their teeth with twigs and a paste made with rock salt, mint or pepper c.63 days ago. The first modern toothbrushes had pigs' hair bristles and were used in China c.7 days ago.

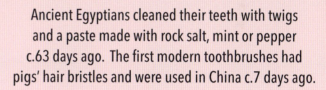

Many modern homes still have open fires. In the future, more homes will be warmed by heat pumps, or solar panels that use energy from the Sun to make electricity.

Heat pumps take heat from the air or from underground, and like boilers, pump it around the house.

12 hours ago first house heated by solar energy

The ancient Egyptians had pet cats more than 100 days ago.

What are your clothes made of? Our early ancestors wore animal hides and woven grasses to protect their skin from the sun and to keep warm at night. We still need to protect our bodies, but we also want to feel comfortable, look smart or express ourselves through what we wear. How did we get from animal hides to catwalk collections?

More than 100 days ago, our clothes were made from natural skins and linen, a fabric made from the flax plant. Very few ancient clothes have survived, because natural fabric rots quickly or is eaten by animals.

More than 100 days ago
cloth made from natural fibres

Skirts were originally worn by men. The oldest known skirt was found in Armenia and was made of straw.

In South America, Asia and Africa, c.55 days ago, people discovered that the fluffy, white fruit of the cotton plant could be woven into a warm, lightweight material.

The oldest known garment is a long shirt or dress made of linen, from ancient Egypt.

The world's oldest known woolly jumper was found in Norway.

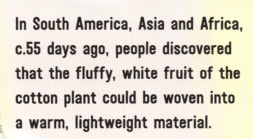

In ancient China, c.56 days ago, silk cloth was first woven from the silky threads that unravel from the cocoons of silk worms.

The first cotton jeans were made for miners in the USA.

When the spinning frame was invented, about two days and six hours ago, it completely changed the way clothes were made. Huge machines spun fibres and wove cloth, without the help of a human hand. The clothes industry transformed again around 21 hours ago, when synthetic fabrics made from chemicals and oil were invented. For the first time in history, coats, dresses and trousers made of nylon or polyester could be made quickly and cheaply, changing fashion forever.

Basketball shoes made of canvas (cotton) and human-made rubber were invented in the USA.

The first mini-skirts were made of polyester, a human-made fabric.

20 hours ago
nylon, a human-made fibre, first worn

Today, more than half of all the clothes in the world are made from synthetic fabrics. We don't repair clothes as we used to, and very few are recycled.

How do you connect with your friends?

Do you write notes or send text messages? Our ancestors didn't have pens or devices – they painted pictures on cave walls and told stories that were passed down over generations.

Around 54 days ago, writing appeared. It allowed people to record language and pass on their ideas and knowledge. Writing is one of humankind's greatest achievements. How did it begin?

54 days ago
first writing
(cuneiform)

One of the first cities was Ur in modern Iraq. Officials there invented a style of writing called cuneiform as a way of recording who owned property.

The King of Uruk wrote the first story ever recorded. The story, called the *Epic of Gilgamesh*, was carved in cuneiform on 12 stone tablets.

Then, c.53 days ago, the ancient Egyptians developed a more complicated writing system called hieroglyphics, which used pictures to represent sounds, syllables and words.

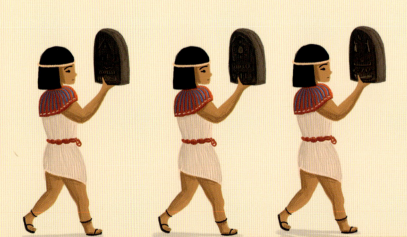

The first paper was made in China, c.19 days ago. Later, the Chinese made books using hand-carved wooden blocks and ink to print each page. Each book took years to make.

Johannes Gutenberg invented the printing press in Germany nearly six days ago. At last, books could be printed quickly, which meant knowledge, ideas and music were shared more widely than ever before.

Newspapers, radio, the telegraph, telephone, photography, film and television are all part of the massive transformation in global communications that changed the way we connect and share information.

When Tim Berners-Lee invented the World Wide Web (c.8 hours ago), suddenly people could send information anywhere in the world, through the internet. Now many of us do this with smartphones and, like the ancient Egyptians, we still use images to communicate, only now we call them emojis!

The first smartphone released was called The Simon Personal Communicator.

6 hours ago
first text message and smartphone

Do you like music? Playing music and singing is something that so many people love to do. Music allows us to share feelings, capture moods, and communicate without using words. We don't know when music was first played, but more than 100 days ago, our ancestors beat drums and played flutes made from animal bone. Flutes, drums and horns are ancient musical instruments that you will still hear in an orchestra today.

More than **100** days ago first musical instruments

The drum appears in many cultures and is one of the earliest musical instruments.

Young boys at school in ancient Greece learned to play a stringed instrument called the kithara.

The benet was an early harp played in ancient Egypt.

The oldest known flute was carved from the bone of a vulture.

We have created many different styles of music, with all the instruments people have invented, from classical and jazz, to rock, reggae, pop and rap. For most of our existence, if you wanted to hear music, you had to listen to a live band or play it yourself. But records, radio and television changed all of that. Today, we can also make music on computers and share it with millions of people around the world almost instantly.

The ancient Egyptian memet was a wooden instrument with a single reed. It is the ancestor of the clarinet and the saxophone.

The ancient Celts of Europe played the carnyx – a long, bronze, trumpet-like tube shaped like an S. Like the memet and benet, this instrument is no longer played.

When Adolphe Sax combined the reed of the clarinet with the brass bell of the trumpet, he invented the saxophone (c.1 day and 14 hours ago).

17 hours and 15 mins ago
first digital music

Music stored as a sequence of numbers on a computer is digital. The first digital music that we can still hear today was a children's nursery rhyme.

Have you ever had a headache? If you have, a doctor or an adult may have given you medicine. But if you had a throbbing headache 90 days ago, someone might have drilled a hole in your head, to release the evil spirits. This is called trepanning. Thanks to modern medicine, we have developed other ways of treating headaches.

90 days ago, headaches 'cured' by trepanning

TREPANNING

Our ancestors practised trepanning, and amazingly, people survived! Now we know that headaches happen for many reasons, but evil spirits aren't the cause.

ACUPUNCTURE

Acupuncture is a type of medicine in which tiny needles are placed along energy lines on the body. It was first practised in ancient China at least 45 days ago.

About 24 days ago, Hippocrates (an ancient Greek physician) was the first person to describe very bad headaches called migraines. He treated his patients with medicine extracted from plants.

HERBAL REMEDIES

Poppy flowers and extract of willow tree were well-known painkillers in ancient Greece.

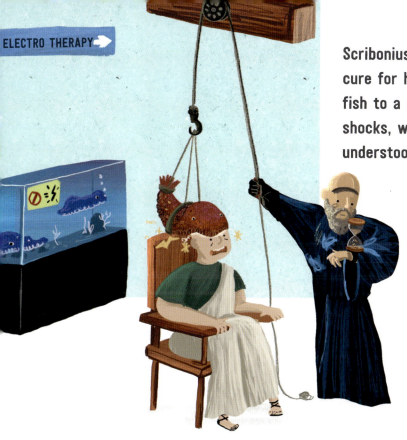

ELECTRO THERAPY →

Scribonius Largus, a physician in ancient Rome, had a shocking cure for headaches c.20.5 days ago. He attached a live torpedo fish to a patient's head. The fish, which produced electric shocks, was left there until the pain went away. Largus understood that small electric currents can treat headaches.

Felix Hoffman, a German chemist, created aspirin in his laboratory and discovered that it was a very effective way of dealing with headaches.

DISPENSARY ←

1 day and 6 hours ago headaches relieved with aspirin

One of the chemicals in aspirin is similar to a chemical found in willow bark.

WAITING ROOM →

Today, adults all over the world still take aspirin when they have a headache, or they may be treated with acupuncture. In severe cases, a patient may need an operation on their brain. Then, the patient is put to sleep and a surgeon drills a hole into the skull. This is a modern form of trepanning.

Do you think the wheel is important?

Look around and you'll see that wheels are everywhere. Some people say the wheel is the most important invention of all time because it had a huge effect on transport, farming and industry. But the very first wheels were actually made of stone and were used to make clay pots.

Before the wheel was used for transport, our ancestors walked everywhere, rode on beasts, and built boats to cross the seas. The invention of the wooden wheel and axle (a shaft that turns a wheel) allowed people to travel and move goods further and faster than ever before.

Wheels with spokes were lighter and faster, and made chariots easier to turn.

Stephan Farffler, a German clockmaker, broke his back as a child. He used his clockmaking skills to build the first self-propelling wheelchair c.3.5 days ago.

46 days ago
the first chariot

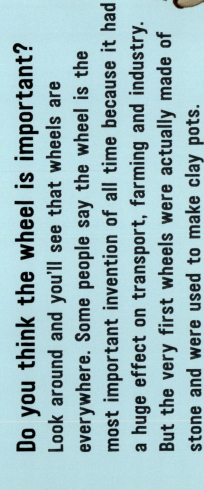

Solid wooden wheels were used on carts, and then chariots, in ancient Iraq and Europe.

The first passenger steam train was invented by George Stephenson c.1 day and 18 hours ago. The 'Locomotive' was supported by four large iron wheels and powered by coal.

A busy city needs transport. The omnibus was invented in the city of Nantes, in France, c.1 day and 17 hours ago. People hopped on and off the bus at different stops.

The first bicycle (c. 1 day and 10 hours ago), called the velocipede, had wheels made of wood and was called a 'boneshaker'.

Orville and Wilbur Wright were given a toy helicopter when they were boys. They played with it until it broke, but they became obsessed with flight. When they grew up, the brothers made the first flight – in an aeroplane that had altered bicycle wheels (c. 1 day and 4 hours ago).

A Scottish engineer called Robert Thomson invented the pneumatic tyre (filled with air) c. 1.5 days ago. It made travel by carriage faster and more comfortable.

The first motor car was invented in Germany (c. 1 day and 6 hours ago) by Carl Benz. It allowed people to travel long distances overland.

The Sunbeam was the first car to go over 200 miles per hour (322 kilometres per hour). This was c. 1 day ago.

1 day ago
a wheel that changes shape

Wheels that turn into triangular tracks allow a vehicle to adapt to almost any type of landscape. They were invented by the National Robotics and Engineering team at Carnegie Mellon University, USA.

Do you want to travel into space?

If you do, you are not the first person. Humankind has been gazing at the night sky since we first walked on Earth. For most of our history, we believed that planet Earth was the centre of the Universe. Now we know there is no centre, but the Universe did have a beginning – we call it the Big Bang.

It has taken us thousands of years to track the movements of the Moon, planets and stars, and to understand Earth's place in the Universe. But space travel has happened only very recently: astronomers and scientists had to discover the science first. Then engineers had to develop the tools that allowed us to build engines and power rockets to overcome gravity and leave Earth.

The James Webb Space Telescope (JWST) mission is one of the most recent attempts by humankind to understand the Universe. The mission wouldn't be possible without all the scientific discoveries and voyages that happened before. Those discoveries began when someone first decided to watch the stars and record what they saw.

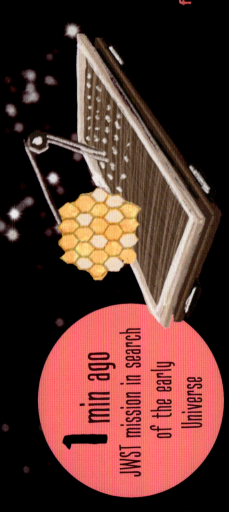

1 min ago
JWST mission in search of the early Universe

The JWST will travel more than 1.5 million kilometres from Earth, to investigate the first stars and galaxies that formed after the Big Bang.

The International Space Station is a base for astronauts to live and work in space. It launched almost 6 hours ago.

Has Earth's temperature changed?

In a word, YES! Earth's temperature has changed many times. There have been cold periods, known as ice ages, when the amount of ice at the poles increased and sea levels dropped. There have been warmer periods too, when ice at the poles melted and shrank. When that happened, Earth's temperature rose and so did sea levels.

One hundred days ago, when people first began to build permanent homes, ice covered much of the planet.

After the last ice age had ended (more than a hundred days ago), Earth slowly warmed and plants began to grow further north. Wild animals and our ancestors began to move north, too.

More than 100 days ago last ice age ended

We are living at a time when there are permanent ice caps around the north and south poles, but the rest of Earth's surface is mostly ice-free. This is called an inter-glacial period. The cycle of cooling and warming on Earth is natural and has happened many times over millions of years.

Carbon dioxide is one of the greenhouse gases in Earth's atmosphere that traps energy from the Sun. Greenhouse gases help keep our planet warm enough to live on.

Because of human activity, Earth is warming faster than at any other time in our history. Many of our factories, power plants and vehicles are powered by fossil fuels such as coal and oil, or by electricity made from burning fossil fuels. When we cut down forests and burn fossil fuels, more carbon dioxide is produced, which changes Earth's natural greenhouse. More heat is trapped and the planet warms up.

The rise in Earth's temperature is called global warming. This is causing sea water to warm and expand, and ice to melt at the poles, which makes sea levels rise. People who live by the coast are at risk from flooding. Global warming also leads to extreme weather events such as droughts and wildfires.

2 days ago
Earth begins to warm up because of human activity

Sea levels have risen almost 20 centimetres on average in recent years and Earth's temperature has risen by 1.1 degrees Celsius.

Has this progress been good? Mostly, yes. Settling down has allowed us to produce enough food to feed billions of people. We have built homes, and cities with hospitals and schools, and created beautiful art. Medicines exist that help us live longer, and technologies allow us to communicate worldwide and to travel into space. We also have time to think, play and learn.

Have there been negative effects? Unfortunately, yes. In many places, the natural environment has been destroyed through farming and city building. The piles of waste we create in our cities are breeding grounds for disease.

What will the future look like? We don't know for certain. World population is still growing, and by 2100, there may be 10.5 billion people. Our planet will be more crowded and more cities will become megacities.

In **1.5** hours' time, there may be 2.5 billion more people on the planet

How will we get around? There will be more self-driving vehicles and they will run on electricity, rather than fossil fuels. But, we will probably drive less. Instead, virtual-reality (VR) systems could allow us to experience all of the sights and sounds of travelling around the world, without leaving our living rooms.

Will technology change? It will play an even bigger part in our lives than it does today. We already have computers that know how to think and learn (this is called artificial intelligence or AI), but one day we may control devices using our thoughts. Some of our clothes, too, will come with technology built in. They may monitor our health and repair themselves, and babies' clothes may grow with them!

Where will most of us live? As cities grow bigger, buildings will grow taller. In countries where there isn't a lot of space, city planners and architects are building up in to the sky, bringing green spaces with them. And where countries are at risk of flooding because of rising sea-levels caused by climate change, we may build floating island cities.

What will the world look like 100 days from now (around the year 12000)? Will all people still live on Earth? Astronauts already live in space but will there be bases or cities on the Moon or Mars? It won't happen soon, but it might happen one day.

This timeline shows you when things happened in actual years. It starts with the first human beings, like us, and includes some of the major events and discoveries covered in this book. The early years are approximate. Our book begins at 8000BCE*.

8000 BCE world population reaches 7.24 million

100 days ago

c.300,000BCE *Homo sapiens*, first modern human beings

c.40,000BCE oldest known flute (Germany)

c.10,000BCE people settle and begin to farm

c.7500BCE first cities (Iraq, Turkey, Palestine)

1886 motor car, invented by Carl Benz (Germany)

1876 telephone Alexander G. Bell (UK)

1844 first message sent by telegraph

1825 first steam train (UK)

1804 world population reaches 1 billion

2 days ago

1767 First spinning frame for weaving cloth (UK)

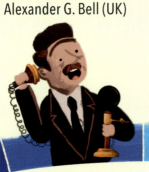  

1903 Wright brothers, first aeroplane flight (USA)

1927 Georges Lemaître, Big Bang Theory (Belgium)

1928 colour TV broadcast (UK)

1939 nylon tights, first human-made (oil-based) fabric (USA)

1951 first digital music (Australia and UK)

1961 Yuri Gagarin, first person to orbit Earth (former USSR, now Russia)

* BCE means Before the Common Era (the birth of Jesus Christ). CE means after the Common Era.

Think about some of the inventions that changed the world, such as the wheel, the printing press, the compass, medicine, space rockets and the World Wide Web. What will we invent in the next 100 days, and how will those things change the way we live?